3/6

be filled

NOW

D1419163

be filled
NOW

by

ROY HESSION

'Be filled with the Spirit'
(Eph. 5. 18)

CHRISTIAN LITERATURE CRUSADE
LONDON

CHRISTIAN LITERATURE CRUSADE
106A Church Road, London, S.E.19

U.S.A.
Fort Washington, Pa.

AUSTRALIA
110 Vittoria Road, Eastwood, N.S.W.

NEW ZEALAND
Box 1688, Auckland, C.1

also in
Europe, Canada,
Central America, South America
West Indies, Africa, India,
Indonesia, Far East

Printed in Great Britain by Richard Clay (The Chaucer Press), Ltd.,
Bungay, Suffolk

CONTENTS

CONTENTS

CHAPTER ONE

NOW—NOT TOMORROW

'BE filled—Now' is more than the title of this small book. It actually summarises in three words the heart of the message of grace to which these chapters lead. It is not, be filled tomorrow, when we hope we shall have improved, but be filled *now* in the midst of our failure and current need—as we are, where we are. And after this now, the next now. Such an experience of present-tense blessedness for needy people can only be possible as we are given a new sight of the grace of God making every blessing available on street level. It is in this context we are to hear the word, 'be filled with the Spirit'.

The place and function of the Holy Spirit in the life of the individual believer and of the Church as a whole is vastly important. If it is a basic truth of the Christian faith that no man can know God except in the face of Jesus Christ (John 1. 18; 2 Cor. 4. 6), it is also true that no man can see that face and acknowledge Him as Lord except by the revelation of the Holy Spirit (1 Cor. 12. 3). Moreover, the apostolic injunction, 'Be filled with the Spirit' (Eph. 5. 18) still stands binding on every believer, and he ignores it at the peril of missing the fruitfulness and joy which such fulness brings.

In treating this subject of being filled with the Holy Spirit, I have avoided dealing with the matter of the gifts of the Spirit, such as speaking in tongues, healing and the like (1 Cor. 12. 8–10). This may seem strange in view of the current widespread interest among Christians in this subject, and the fact that an increasing number in many denominations across the world now are testifying to receiving an experience of the Holy Spirit to the accompaniment of such manifestations and gifts. Any new writing on the subject of the Holy Spirit might be bound to take cognisance of this fact and have much to say about it. To omit this side may seem to make such a writing irrelevant to the current movements in the Church; it even might make some feel frustrated and impatient, for this seems to be what so many want to hear about. I have however omitted doing so quite purposely, and that for two reasons.

First, the experience of the supernatural gifts of the Spirit tends to divide Christians into two groups, (dare we say it?) the 'haves' and the 'have nots'. Satan can tempt us either to despise one another or to disagree with one another. The message of the grace of God in the present tense, however, is for both. The one who has had experience of the gifts of the Spirit may yet need to learn how to go on being filled with the Spirit, when sin and falling short have brought dryness. In such times the memory of great experiences in the past will do nothing to help him—rather it may depress him. He needs to see the grace of God perfectly adapted to his need, and that continuously, and come again as a sinner. On the other hand, the one who cannot claim to have had these experiences need not feel himself deprived on that account. The grace of God is like an ocean of water ever seeking depth, that is need, that it might fill it. The true meaning of grace is the *undeserved* love of God. The emphasis must always be on the fact that it is undeserved, if grace is to be grace. That being so, the only qualification to make us fit candidates for that grace is, not the possessing of this or that gift, but need fully and frankly confessed. As we have said, grace makes the fulness of the Spirit available for both groups on street level, at the foot of the Cross.

The other reason is that quite obviously from Paul's writing in his first epistle to the Corinthians, speaking in tongues and the other gifts, though recognised and given their place, are incidental, not the heart of the Spirit-filled life. My purpose has been to leave aside for the time being that which is incidental, and to share only what I see to be inward and essential. And here I write only as a learner and a fellow-discoverer of the grace of God and the fulness of the Spirit.

CHAPTER TWO

THE HOLY SPIRIT A PERSON

THIS chapter will be a short one and will cover ground which every instructed Christian should know. But it is necessary for us to lay the foundation first of all, so that we can begin together.

The Holy Spirit is not to be regarded merely as an influence. He is a Person, the third Person of the Trinity, as much a Person as God the Father and God the Son. He is consistently referred to in the New Testament not as it, but as He. The one place where the Authorised Version refers to 'the Spirit itself' (Rom. 8. 16), the Revised Version rightly changes, in the interests of greater accuracy of translation, to 'The Spirit *himself* beareth witness with our spirit that we are children of God'. In another place the writer violates the normal principles of grammar to make sure that the Spirit is referred to as a Person. The passage is John 16. 13, where we have the words, 'When he, the Spirit of truth, is come'. The Greek word translated Spirit is *pneuma*; which is a neuter word, and yet, contrary to what one would expect grammatically, the personal pronoun, He, is linked with it.

Thus at the outset we would bow in worship before this august member of the Godhead. To Him is committed the carrying out of all the designs of heaven with regard to earth. The Father has given all authority to the Son (Matt. 28. 18), but the actual implementing of that authority on earth is the work of the Holy Spirit. He is the executive of the Godhead and in that capacity we see Him moving and acting right through the Book of Acts, which could be more accurately termed the Acts of the Holy Spirit rather than the Acts of the Apostles.

We have spoken of the designs of heaven with regard to earth. The first great design is that every man who has repented of his sins and put his faith in the Lord Jesus Christ should be given a second birth and be made a new creature. This is the special sphere of the Holy Spirit, for He is the agent of our new birth (John 3. 8). He does this by coming personally to take up residence in the heart of the one who ventures his faith on Christ, and to abide there for ever (John 14. 16).

> *Soon as my all I ventured*
> *On the atoning Blood,*
> *The Holy Spirit entered,*
> *And I was born of God.*

This is the one thing that distinguishes the child of God from everybody else—he has 'received, not the spirit of the world, but the spirit which is of God' (1 Cor. 2. 12).

It cannot be too clearly stated, then, that every man who has been born anew through faith in Christ has received the Holy Spirit. Indeed, the Spirit's presence in our hearts is said in Ephesians 1 to be the seal that we are Christ's. 'In whom also after that ye believed, ye were sealed with that holy Spirit of promise.' Without this seal, Romans 8. 9 tells us, we are 'none of his'. But the Ephesians passage tells us that the Holy Spirit is not only the seal, but also 'the earnest of our inheritance until the redemption of the purchased possession'. An earnest simply means a down-payment, (for thus the Amplified New Testament translates this word). So the Holy Spirit in our hearts is the seal of what is Christ's and the down-payment of what will be ours one day in glory. If the down-payment means 'joy unspeakable and full of glory', what will the final instalment be?

Quite clearly then, the further experiences of fulness and empowerment there are for us through the Holy Spirit cannot properly be called a receiving of the Holy Spirit, for how can we receive Him whom we have already received? The references in the New Testament to receiving the Holy Spirit (such as Gal. 3. 2) can therefore only refer to that initial receiving of the Spirit at our new birth.

What then is to be filled with the Holy Spirit? It is simply to be filled with One who is already there, in our hearts. Let me give an illustration of the difference between the Holy Spirit being initially in the believer, and the same Holy Spirit filling him. Take up a sponge and while it is in your hand squeeze it. In that condition, plunge it in water and submerge it, keeping it there. It is now in the water and the water is in it, though only in a small degree. As you hold it in the water, you open your hand; and as you do so the water fills all the pores which you release in this way. It is now filled with the water. In the same way when we come to know Jesus Christ as Saviour and are born anew we are put into that sphere where the Holy Spirit is operating and the Holy Spirit comes to reside within us. That is what Paul means when he says, 'Ye are not in the flesh, but in the Spirit, if so be that the Spirit of God dwell in you' (Rom. 8. 9). Yes, we are in the Spirit, and the Spirit is in us. But that Holy Spirit may not be in full control of us. We may yet need to be filled with the Spirit in whom we have been placed. We are therefore to open up every part of our being to Him, giving in to His conviction and yielding to His lordship. And as we do so, we are filled with the Spirit. We are not only in the Spirit, but now the Spirit is very fully in us.

This is, however, anticipating an aspect of our theme to which we shall come later more fully. At this point let us pause in wonder at the glorious fact that, if we have come in repentance and faith to the Lord Jesus, the august Holy Spirit Himself is in us by His Spirit, making our bodies His own temples.

CHAPTER THREE

THE HOLY SPIRIT THE ADVOCATE
OF THE LORD JESUS

WE may now turn to consider what is the function or work of the Holy Spirit here on earth.

The Lord Jesus referred to Him on a number of occasions as 'the Comforter' (John 14. 16, 26; 15. 26) and told the disciples that it was expedient that He, the Lord Jesus, should go away, for otherwise the Comforter would not come unto them (John 16. 7). This word 'Comforter' will help us to understand His function among us. It is the same word in the Greek (*paraclete*) as appears in 1 John 2. 1, where it is translated 'Advocate'; 'If any man sin, we have an advocate with the Father, Jesus Christ the righteous; and he is the propitiation for our sins.' Therefore it would be quite in order to substitute the word 'Advocate' for the word 'Comforter' with regard to the Holy Spirit. This means there are two Advocates referred to in these passages; the one is the Lord Jesus Christ and the other is the Holy Spirit.

An advocate is, as we know, one who looks after our interests in a court of law, and answers for us. Here we have a picture of the work of the Lord Jesus for us. He is our Advocate in heaven, and as such, He delights to look after the repentant sinner's interests in those awesome courts. He does not attempt to produce evidence to show our innocence. He knows that every accusation of the holy law of God against us is true, but he pleads on our behalf the value of His atoning Blood. When we sin, our Advocate presents Himself to the Father as the propitiation for our sins. As the hymn says, 'He shows His wounds and spreads His hands'. But for the heavenly intercession of his Advocate, every child of God would have lost his relationship with the Father long ago. However, he does lose his sense of peace with God when he sins. But as he confesses his sin, he has a renewal of that peace with

God through the Blood of Jesus, which he knew when he first came to Him. How wonderful to have a Friend at court like this!

In this passage in John, however, the Holy Spirit is also called an Advocate. This Advocate is not resident in heaven, but in the hearts of believers with whom He comes to dwell when they are born again. But whose Advocate is He? Not the believer's Advocate but rather the Saviour's, whose interests He is charged to safeguard. Here then are the two Advocates, the believer's Advocate with the Father which is Christ, and Christ's Advocate with the believer which is the Holy Spirit. The One looks after the believer's interests in heaven; the Other looks after Christ's interests in the believer.

This makes quite clear His great function. It is to safeguard the interests and throne rights of the Lord Jesus in the world, the Church and the individual believer. This is precisely what the Lord Jesus meant when He said of the Holy Spirit, 'He shall glorify me' (John 16. 14). His work is to represent Christ, to speak of Christ, to exalt Christ, to deal with men with regard to Christ, to convict them of sin because they have not believed on Christ, to cause them to repent because of the place they have not given to Christ. Christ, Christ, Christ is the theme of all His speech and the direction of all His activity.

But the Lord not only said of Him, 'He shall glorify me', but also 'He shall receive of mine, and shall shew it unto you' (John 16. 14). This simply means surely that having brought us to repentance with regard to Christ, He will show us the resources of Christ to deal with our now acknowledged sinfulness.

> *Spirit of God my Teacher be,*
> *Showing the things of Christ to me.*

And these 'things' are the things concerning His grace for the guilty, His love for the unlovely, the completeness of His redemption and the value of His Blood and righteousness for people as bad as we now acknowledge ourselves to be—indeed the sufficiency of Jesus for every possible need. They are the 'things' that make for the sinner's peace and pardon, for the Lord Jesus came into the world to save such. It is quite obviously the work of His Advocate to show to penitent ones the complete adequacy of His resources to that end. Indeed, nowhere does the Spirit so glorify Christ as when He reveals the riches of His grace for failures who acknowledge their failure. The recovery of human failure is the sphere where Jesus Christ excels, where He gets His Name. He is not shocked by sin, nor defeated by it, for this is the realm where grace finds its opportunity and He has the answer for it. The convicted one would never believe it, did not the Holy Spirit reveal it to him. How glorious does the Saviour become in his eyes under the Spirit's ministry!

Here then is the Holy Spirit as the great Advocate of the Lord Jesus, to make known to us our need and the rich provisions in Jesus to meet that need. Well has A. H. Vine put it in his hymn to the Holy Spirit,

> *Christ is our Advocate on high,*
> *Thou art our Advocate within,*
> *O plead the truth and make reply*
> *To ev'ry argument of sin.*

It might be however better to say that the Holy Spirit is not *our* Advocate, but *Christ's* Advocate, for it is as such that He 'pleads the truth and makes reply to every argument of sin', pointing to Christ and His Blood as the answer.

A vivid illustration of the position and work of the Holy Spirit in God's dealings with men is contained in the story of Abraham sending his servant to a distant land to seek a bride for his son, Isaac. If that servant had spoken of himself and fixed men's eyes there, he would have failed of his object. Having found the right girl, his real work was only just begun. It was so to speak of his master's son as to draw her heart to that son and make her willing to break with her family and follow him to Isaac. Morning, noon and night there was but one theme to his conversation, 'my master's son'. His appearance and attractiveness were doubtless enlarged upon, but especially his wealth, for 'unto him hath my master given all that he hath'. The earrings and bracelets with which he had decked her were but specimens of the wealth that would be the girl's who consented to become his wife. He was apparently a highly eligible young man! 'And it came to pass' when Laban, Rebecca's brother, 'saw the earrings and bracelets upon his sister's hands . . . he said, "Come in, thou blessed of the Lord; wherefore standest thou without?" ' 'Come in,' he said in effect, 'and tell us more about your master's son.' And so he was given ample scope to exercise his ministry. In no time at all, the girl's heart was won and she gave her answer. 'I will go.' The servant's joy was fulfilled when at last he saw Rebecca in Isaac's arms!

The work of the blessed Holy Spirit is precisely to play the part with us that Abraham's servant played with them long ago—so to speak of Christ and of grace and of glory as to woo and win our hearts and make us willing to follow Him to Calvary, there to take the sinner's place at the feet of Jesus. And He does this not only to bring about our first meeting with Jesus, but continually ever after, whenever sin has made us cold and dry and barren. How good it is that Jesus has not left Himself without an Advocate on earth to represent Him in our hearts and to draw us back again and again to His Cross, the place of release and victory.

The Holy Spirit, then, has but one purpose, to exalt Christ. A grasp and experience of this fundamental fact will save us from all sorts of mistakes and sometimes from being dangerously side-tracked. If an outstanding experience of the Holy Spirit leads us to exalt the Holy Spirit and to centre on that experience, then we will find that instead of co-operating with the Holy Spirit we are actually thwarting Him in His design to direct man's eyes on the Lord Jesus alone.

CHAPTER FOUR

THE HOLY SPIRIT THE CONVICTER

FOR simplicity's sake we can divide the Holy Spirit's work as the Advocate of the Lord Jesus into two.

First of all, He comes to reprove or convict us of sin and bring us to repentance. Jesus said, 'When he is come, he will reprove the world of sin ... because they believe not on me' (John 16. 8–9). Three times in the well-known chapters in John on the Holy Spirit (chapters 14, 15 and 16), He is called by the Lord Jesus 'the Spirit of truth'. Truth here does not mean a body of doctrine, but the revelation of facts as they really are. This means that it is the work of the Holy Spirit to reveal to us the truth about ourselves as sinners. Silently and inexorably He is shining the white light of truth all the time on the thoughts and reactions of our hearts, the words of our lips and the deeds of our hands. Everything which is of self-centredness and sin is revealed as such, no matter how we dress it up and rationalise it. He is concerned to shatter the realm of illusion about ourselves in which we have been living, and bring us to true self-knowledge. His great concern is that we should know the truth for He is the Spirit of truth. The response He requires is simply the response of honesty which says 'Truth, Lord' (Matt. 15. 27) to all He shows us about ourselves, without self-excuse or hiding anything. This is what is meant by 'Thou desirest truth in the inward parts' in Psa. 51. The same phrase, 'Thou desirest' comes a little further down the same Psalm, only this time it is 'Thou desirest not sacrifice'. Put these two together and you discover the message of the Psalm, 'Thou desirest not sacrifice but truth in the inward parts'. So often activity, even Christian service, can be a cloke to hide the truth both from ourselves and from others. The Holy Spirit is against all such self-deception and sham. It is truth and not sacrifice which He requires in such a case.

This is what is meant too by the phrase 'doeth truth' in John 3. 21. There we read that whereas he that does evil hates the light, neither comes to the light lest his deeds should be reproved, it is he that does truth who comes to the light that his deeds may be made manifest that they are wrought in God. We would have thought that the opposite of 'doing evil' would be doing good, but not with God. With Him the opposite of doing evil is 'doing truth', that is honesty about our evil. Before we ever try to do good where we have done evil, He wants a full exposure to Him of that evil, a simple saying of 'Truth, Lord' to what He is showing us. He would much rather have us turn back the past leaves than turn over a new leaf, for when we turn over a new leaf we of necessity hide the former leaf, and when sin is hidden the Blood of Jesus cannot cleanse us nor we ourselves be brought to peace. The promise of forgiveness and cleansing is conditioned on simply confessing our sins (1 John 1. 9). We do not have to ask for forgiveness if we have confessed our sins. We get it on the spot the moment we confess. But all the asking in the world will not bring peace to our hearts if there is a reservation in our confession. This is so not only between man and God but it is also seen to be ineffectual between man and man. Who of us have not found ourselves saying to another in our attempt to get right with him something like, 'Please forgive me if I have wronged you' and wondered why it did nothing to heal the breach. There is no 'if'; let us confess we *have* wronged him, and we may be surprised at the speed at which the grace of God reaches us, and very often the forgiveness of man too.

This then is the conviction of the Holy Spirit, the shining of the light of truth, and the response of truth which is required of us. And this shining of the light of truth is going on all the time, as silently and as inexorably as the shining of the sun. It is surely inconceivable that the Holy Spirit only convicts of sin at special seasons of spiritual awakening, and is content to let us off at other times. There is no 'out of season' time for the Holy Spirit. If we have not been conscious of conviction of sin, it is not because He

B

has not been convicting, but rather because we have not been willing to hear and to see. It is easy to avoid conviction of sin, for the Spirit's voice is gentle. Only those who are eager to be convicted will hear His voice, and they only will be eager because they hunger for the Lord Jesus and know that this is the only way by which they will be freed from the things that separate them from Him, whom they have begun to love.

Sometimes we are in a condition where no conviction seems to come to us and we think all must be well. Then we might meet some other Christians who are praising God with a fresh testimony of how the Spirit has convicted them on some particular point and the Blood of Jesus has cleansed them at that point. We look on with wonder, feeling that this is not our experience. Is it that we have got beyond the need of being dealt with about such things, or is it that we are just not seeing them as they are? So often it is the latter. And the reason why we are not seeing these. what we may call smaller things, is that there is some larger, more basic matter we are not willing for God to deal with. Let us imagine, to illustrate, a high wall, which casts a strong shadow in the bright sunlight. In that shadow the many weeds growing there are hardly noticed. But when that large wall is removed, the light then shows up the smaller weeds, each one casting its own shadow, and then they can be removed. To 'walk in the light' with God (1 John 1. 7) simply means to say yes to what that light reveals. This may mean the removing of some very real barrier between us and God. But that may not lead to less conviction of sin but rather more, for now the Lord can show us the smaller day-to-day things that spring up so easily from our fallen natures. But conviction is always followed by cleansing if we are quick to say, 'Yes, Lord'.

Notice, however, that in this work of conviction the Holy Spirit is all the time acting as the Advocate of the Lord Jesus, which means that He always speaks to us of our sin in relation to Christ. He does not convict us of sin as something merely unethical or contrary to the ten commandments, but as that which has dethroned the Lord Jesus and caused His death upon the Cross. The Spirit is not content till we have been helped to look upon Him whom we have pierced and mourned for Him. Indeed the nature of sin of which He convicts us is described as 'of sin because they believe not on Me'. This suggests that the larger all-inclusive sin is unbelief, the unwillingness to avail ourselves of the redemption of Christ, and that, in turn, is because of our stiff-necked obstinacy and hardness of heart. He has not been dealing with us very long over something before the issue shifts from the sin in question to the unbroken attitude, the obstinacy and the self-justification we manifest over His dealings.

What an illustration we have of the Spirit's conviction and of our unwillingness in the story of the servants of Naaman pleading with their master when he was unwilling to obey the prophet's word to 'go and wash in Jordan seven times'! He was willing for anything but that. That would have meant stripping, and the extent of his leprosy being seen. But his servants came and pleaded with him so tenderly (for they loved him much), 'My father, if the prophet had bid thee do some great thing, wouldest thou not have done it? how much rather then, when he saith to thee, Wash, and be clean?' (2 Kings 5. 13). How glad he was that he yielded to their gentle entreaties, for his flesh came again like the flesh of a little child. Even so the Holy Spirit holds us gently to the one thing we do not want to do because of our pride, 'Go and wash at the foot of the Cross of Christ.' We fear the stripping that repentance involves us in and that we shall be seen for what we really are. But how glad we are when we do yield, for we emerge cleansed and made whole through the Blood of Christ.

It is clear, then, that in the Spirit's contending with us, He is acting all the time as the Advocate of the Lord Jesus, only desiring that we should bow our heads to Him and acknowledge Him King on the new point at issue.

CHAPTER FIVE

THE HOLY SPIRIT THE COMFORTER

HAVING seen the Holy Spirit as the convicter of those who sin, we now need to see Him as the Comforter of those who repent. The moment the Spirit succeeds in breaking us in repentance, the whole direction of His ministry seems to change—it is directed wholly to comforting the now contrite one and encouraging him to find everything in Christ. To a people who had 'received of the Lord's hand double for all their sins', the message was of old, 'Comfort ye, comfort ye my people, saith your God' (Isa. 40. 1). And so it is today.

If the translators used the word 'Comforter', it is because the Greek word bears that meaning as much as 'Advocate', and those who know the Holy Spirit's work in their hearts know how worthily He bears that name. He who is so relentless and disconcerting in His conviction of sin is wonderfully sweet in the comfort He gives the one who mourns for sin and laments his poverty. 'Blessed are they that mourn,' said Jesus, 'for they shall be comforted,' and it is the Holy Spirit who applies that comfort. And He does so by taking the things of Christ and showing them unto us (John 16. 14). This simply means that to the repentant heart He witnesses of Christ and of the sufficiency of His precious Blood for his peace and right standing with God, and bids him believe in Him afresh and rejoice. He reveals that the sins which we confess were anticipated and settled by the Lord Jesus on the Cross before they were even committed, that provision has been made ahead of time for the very poverty in which we find ourselves. He witnesses of a risen Saviour showing us that God has set the seal of His infinite satisfaction upon the atoning work of our Lord by raising Him again from the dead, and that if God is satisfied with His work on our behalf, we may be too. He witnesses to the struggling saint hoping for improvement in the flesh, that the man who commits these sins (the 'old man' of Romans 6 which merely means the 'man of old') was judicially crucified with Christ (that is, in God's sight ended, not mended). He may therefore cease to be disappointed in a man whom God has brought to an end in the Cross, and may turn wholly to Christ who is made to him all he needs. And as the Spirit thus witnesses to him, he is enabled to believe the blessed record, and he is free in spirit, rejoicing with joy and full of glory for such a wonderful salvation.

> *I know not how the Spirit moves,*
> *Convincing men of sin,*
> *Revealing Jesus in His Word*
> *Creating faith in Him.*

We may not know how He does it—sometimes through some word of Scripture, or through another's testimony, or the line of a hymn, or in more direct and inexplicable ways—but we may certainly know He does it, for this is His great work in the Church.

We seem to appreciate most intensely the Spirit's ministry as Comforter, when, having become cold and out of touch with God, we try to get back to Him by 'works'. How natural it is for us to imagine that if we have got away from Him by committing sin, we shall come back to Him by doing good. And so we promise ourselves we will try harder, we set ourselves higher goals, we seek to do more for God or even to spend longer on our devotions. All these things are right, of course, but inasmuch as we so often do not attain those goals, we only end by burdening ourselves with additional self-reproach and an added sense of failure. We become tense in our efforts to improve, and condemned because we cannot succeed. We have come to experience what Paul did, when he said, 'The commandment, which was ordained to life (if I could attain to it), I found to be unto death (because I failed to do so),' and if we go farther along this road, we shall be in the same place of despair that he came to when he said, 'O wretched man that I am! who shall deliver me from the body of this death?' (Rom. 7. 10 and 24). What a relief it is when the Holy

Spirit points us, as He did Paul, away from our work to Another's work, the finished work of Christ for us on the Cross, whereby we see that the work has been done for us, the distance between us and God bridged and peace made! The Spirit bids us cease from trying to get peace by our efforts, and to come to Jesus as a sinner and rest in what He had done. As we do so, the burden of striving and self-reproach slips away from our hearts, and the Comforter whispers peace to our hearts.

> *Nothing either great or small,*
> *Nothing sinner, no!*
> *Jesus did it, did it all,*
> *Long, long ago.*

> *Till to Jesus' work you cling,*
> *By a simple faith,*
> *Doing is a deadly thing,*
> *Doing ends in death.*

> *Cast your deadly doing down,*
> *Down at Jesus' feet,*
> *Stand in Him, in Him alone,*
> *Gloriously complete!*

One of the best illustrations of the Spirit's testimony to the finished work of Jesus is that of the dove returning to Noah in the ark, 'And, lo, in her mouth was an olive leaf pluckt off: so Noah knew that the waters were abated from off the earth' (Gen. 8. 11). The testimony that the dove brought back was the olive leaf in its mouth. As Noah saw it, he knew that there was one spot on the earth from which the waters had passed, there was one bit that was clear of judgement, and this was a message of peace to those in the ark. Today the Holy Spirit brings the testimony that there is One Person who is clear of judgement. He was once under it, absolutely so, but He has come out of it in resurrection power. But the judgement of which He is now clear is our judgement. Therefore if our Surety is clear of it, we for whom He stood surety are clear of it too. This is what is meant when it says that

He 'Who was delivered for our offences ... was raised again for our justification' (Rom. 4. 25).

If we want to see the dove with the olive leaf in her mouth, read through the Acts of the Apostles. All the time we see the Holy Spirit is bearing witness to a risen Christ.

'Whom God hath raised up' (2. 24).
'This Jesus hath God raised up' (2. 32).
'Whom God hath raised from the dead' (3. 15).
'Him God raised up the third day' (10. 40), etc., etc.

Over and over again the Spirit presents the blessed fact that Jesus is clear of the judgement He was once under. This means that in God's sight and reckoning we are as clear of the condemnation and reproach (even self-reproach) of sin as He is. He has been under it; the waves and billows have gone over Him; but He is beyond it for ever now, and that 'for our justification'. The Spirit now witnesses with our spirit that we are as clear of it all as He is.

This is the solid comfort which the Holy Spirit brings to the despairing soul that has learnt to repent. If we take that in our hearts we shall obtain a true sense of the love of God as never before. This is the first wave of the Spirit's power in our souls, the first effect of His indwelling, to shed the love of God abroad in our hearts (see Rom. 5. 5), and thus provoke our love for Him in return.

Let us not forget, then, that the Holy Spirit only convicts in order to comfort. It will help us to distinguish His voice from that of the devil. The devil is called the 'accuser of the brethren' and his accusations to the sensitive conscience are sometimes confused with the convictions of the Holy Spirit. But his accusations never have any comfort in view. They are simply 'nagging', which only leads to despair and bondage. Even as you assent to them, you instinctively know that there is never going to be any end to them. He always leads the soul back to Sinai, to the law, to the standards we have not yet attained and thus to despair. The Holy Spirit's convictions, however, are short and sharp, and we know instinctively that if we would bow to them and say 'yes', there is nothing but peace for our souls. If the devil leads us to Sinai, the Holy Spirit always leads us to Calvary. He is ever the sweet messenger of the new covenant of peace for sinners.

The Holy Spirit's comfort, however, does not only deal with the answer of Christ for our sin, but with His whole resources for our every other conceivable need. 'He shall receive of mine, and shall shew it unto you.' If the government of our affairs is on our own shoulders our one concern is that we shall have power adequate for our responsibilities. But if the government is on His shoulders, then the only One who needs to have the power is He, and that the Spirit delights to show us He has. He reveals Him to our hearts, not merely as the One who can overcome the devil, but who has done so already through His Cross. He shows Him to us seated 'In the heavenly places, far above all principality and power' (Eph. 1. 20, 21), and supreme over every opposing force, and ourselves identified with Him there (see Eph. 2. 6). This means that we are not merely on the winning side, but on the side that has already won; we do not fight for victory but from it.

Till we have some such revelation of the Lord Jesus in our problems, we are tense, worried and striving, and things are on top of us. But when, in our hour of need, the Spirit shows us Jesus and the resources that are His, we are free, we see ourselves in Him as 'the head, and not the tail' (Deut. 28. 13) and defeat is banished in the basic realm from which it needs to be banished, the realm of our spirit. Being victorious in spirit we become victorious in the other spheres too, for faith is the victory that overcomes the world (see 1 John 5. 4). And as we go forward with a new boldness and confidence we find God working for us in our situation.

The story is told of how Spurgeon was once burdened and worried about his problems and responsibilities. Suddenly as he was riding in his carriage he kicked his legs in the air and laughed aloud. He says that what brought joy and release to his heart was seeing himself like a fish worrying as to whether there was water enough for it to swim in when all the time it was swimming in the Atlantic Ocean, and such he saw the grace of his Lord to be for all his need. There in that carriage the mighty Advocate of the

Lord Jesus exercised His ministry as Comforter on behalf of a needy servant of God.

This brings us to the whole question of the power of the Holy Spirit for service, for which some of us so ardently long. Here I can only give my own experience. I find that the Holy Spirit endues with power from on high, not by fixing my eyes on that power so that I fervently pray for it, but rather on the Lord Jesus risen from the dead and showing me the power and position which are His. As I see that, I lose my burdens, fears and striving. I find myself made strong in faith again, and endued with the needed heavenly power for the service at hand. Elisha received the double portion of the Spirit which rested on Elijah only when he saw his master ascend into heaven. Then the mantle, symbol of that power, fluttered down to his feet. Only as we allow the Holy Spirit to show us again the adequacy of the Lord Jesus and believingly receive His revelation, will we find ourselves robed with power from on high and going forth with boldness, to see God working with us.

Sometimes in an evangelistic campaign in which I am involved some Christians have said to me, 'Is it not strange how on a certain day the "break" came, after which the whole campaign took a new turn?' It was not strange to me. I knew what happened to a burdened and tense evangelist on the day in question alone in his bedroom—or rather what he was given to see. He saw Jesus crowned with glory and honour with all things under His feet. The waves he thought were over his head, he saw to be under His feet.

So often we are praying for supply, when what the Spirit wants to give us is sight—sight of Jesus, Jesus crowned and victorious.

It may be asked how do we get this new sight of Jesus as and when we need it? Not by trying to get it, nor even, I suggest, by praying for it, but rather by telling God we have not got it. Let us not dissipate our energies for the time being anywhere else but in this one direction. Tell Him you are not seeing Jesus, tell Him you are in bad shape, that you are not free, that you have not peace. Tell Him you are struggling to get by your efforts what deep down you know is a gift, but that you are struggling none the less. Tell Him that today you have not this sight of Jesus, His Blood and His victory that you had yesterday. Make no effort to get it, just tell Him you have not got it. Then allow Him to show you why you do not have it. He may show you dark and un-suspected things, but say yes to Him. All this is what is meant by going to the feet of Jesus, to the foot of His Cross. Such phrases may sound like cliches to some, but they express an awesome and hallowed experience to others. It is there that the Blood of Jesus avails for you. And you will not have been long at His feet before the Holy Spirit arises with healing in His wings, and gives you to see all you need to see of Jesus, and to possess all you need to possess of His fulness.

CHAPTER SIX

FOUR ATTITUDES TO THE HOLY SPIRIT

HAVING seen the place and function of the Holy Spirit among the people of God, we are in a position to ask ourselves what is our attitude to Him; are we allowing Him to do His work of conviction and revealing Jesus to us as all we need?

The New Testament tells us that there are four possible attitudes that we may take up towards Him. The first is to *grieve Him.* 'Grieve not the holy Spirit of God, whereby ye are sealed unto the day of redemption. Let all bitterness, and wrath, and anger, and clamour, and evil speaking, be put away from you, with all malice' (Eph. 4. 30, 31). Sin is that which grieves Him, especially those sins which are mentioned here in the context; bitterness, anger, evil speaking of others, malice and unforgiveness. When we understand that the One whom He has come to reveal to us is called by that precious name of the Lamb, meek and lowly in heart, and that He Himself is likened to the gentle dove, we can see the sort of things that do grieve Him. Whenever we manifest a disposition other than that of the Lamb (sometimes it is far more like that of the lion!) especially in our relationships with others, we cause Him grief. Although we have been forgiven so much ourselves, we sometimes stand on our rights and refuse to forgive another. He cannot go further with us in His work of blessing, until we see these sins and repent of them. For that reason, He proceeds to convict us of them, and strive with us. But it is ever the work of love; our sins do not anger Him, but rather grieve Him.

The second possible attitude that we can adopt towards Him is to *resist Him.* Stephen said to the Jews of his day, 'Ye stiffnecked and uncircumcised in heart and ears, ye do always resist the Holy Ghost: as your fathers did, so do ye' (Acts 7. 51). When He convicts us of sin, we can resist Him. We can refuse to call something sin which He calls sin. We sometimes work out a complete alibi for ourselves, which proves us guiltless. We do so because we know that to say 'yes' to the Spirit's conviction would humble us, for we should have to repent and put the thing right. This is what the scriptures call being 'stiffnecked', and it is indeed a serious condition to be in, and may lead to solemn judgements upon us, if persisted in. 'He, that being often reproved hardeneth his neck, shall suddenly be destroyed, and that without remedy' (Prov. 29. 1). Our resistance to the Holy Spirit's conviction is seen so often in our refusal to accept the challenge of some brother or sister in Christ. We would not mind if His conviction were direct from Himself to our hearts, but very often He uses somebody else's penetrating words to show us our sin. And that makes it doubly hard to receive, because of our pride. But we must receive it none the less, if we are to be blessed.

The third possible attitude is that of *quenching Him*. Says Paul, 'Quench not the Spirit. Despise not prophesyings' (1 Thess. 5. 19, 20).

This is the word concerning the more corporate activities of the Holy Spirit in our midst, as is seen by the phrase that follows, that we are not to despise prophesyings. We quench a fire when we pour water upon it, and we can quench the fire of the Holy Spirit's working in another, in a fellowship, or in a meeting, by 'pouring cold water upon it', by way of discouraging or actually forbidding it. The Holy Spirit demands to have right of way in the assemblies of God's people and in their fellowship. But so often we have a mental picture of the way in which He must work and we forbid all forms of His working which do not conform exactly to our ideas—especially those forms that would seem to by-pass our own pet methods and would seem to make nothing of our own special position. How prone we are to think that, if revival is to come, it must come through the Minister or the Missionary or only through those who have a special training. The Spirit, however, often brings revival through the back door, through someone of no account at all and of little official position. How often has not the Lord Jesus come knocking at the door of a situation, a Church or a Mission Station but the door has been bolted against Him because He did not come through the proper channels or along normal lines, and thus He had sadly to turn away from a situation that needed Him so desperately.

The fourth attitude that we can take to the Spirit's working is to be *filled* with Him. The Epistle of the Ephesians tells us, 'Be not drunk with wine, wherein is excess; but be filled with the Spirit' (Eph. 5. 18). The One whom we were grieving, resisting and quenching is now filling us and possessing us. What a capitulation and what a reversal this implies on our part! We have at last consented to bow to His conviction and call sin, sin. He is now able without hindrance to give us continual sight of Jesus as all we need to our immense joy, release and empowering.

When thinking of this matter of being filled with the Holy Spirit, it is important always to do so in the context of these three other attitudes to the Spirit. If we do not do so, we shall always be regarding the fulness of the Holy Spirit as a special blessing, extra to our inheritance in Christ, and that attitude will lead us only to striving and frustration. If we are not filled with the Spirit at any given moment, it is only because of one thing—sin. Through sin we have grieved Him, and are resisting Him where He has convicted us. Maybe we have been in a dry, unsatisfied condition for years, but it is all due to an accumulation of this same one thing, sin. But we have only to humble ourselves in repentance under the Holy Spirit's conviction, and He will witness in our hearts to Jesus and His Blood, and enable us to believe that His Blood cleanses what we have confessed. *Then where the Blood cleanses, the Holy Spirit fills, and that without further waiting on our part.*

This is clearly illustrated in the ceremonial cleansing of the leper in the book of Leviticus (Lev. 14). First of all, the blood of a sacrificial victim, a lamb, was placed upon his right ear, his right thumb and his right big toe. Then the holy anointing oil, picture to us of the Holy Spirit, was placed upon the blood in those same three places. First the blood, then the oil. And so it is in the experience of the believer. The Holy Spirit does not fill and empower the flesh, that is, unjudged self. He only comes

C

where there has been repentance and where the Blood of Christ has been applied to sin by faith. Such is the value of the precious Blood to God, that, be a man never such a failure, if he has truly repented, that Blood gives him the title to expect the Holy Spirit immediately to fill his heart and life. He need go no further than the foot of the Cross. Right there, where sin is washed away, if his faith will receive it, the Holy Spirit will fill him and his cup will be running over.

I remember when a fellow-worker and myself were taking part in a ministers' conference in Brazil, a young American missionary flew in from his station in the mission aircraft. A great hunger of heart had brought him. In conversation he told us of the barrenness on their station and the defeat in his own life. There had been only one professed conversion in their area in the whole year. The missionaries had got so cold that if one of them would seek to talk seriously about the Lord, the others would jokingly say, 'He's talking like a missionary!' He told us how recently the Lord had begun to work in his heart again and had shown him things of which he must repent to get right with God. In some matters it meant putting things right with his fellow missionaries. He told us how as a result a new fellowship had begun to grow up between the missionaries and there was a new touch of blessing on the work. We suggested he might give his testimony in the meeting that day. He did so, and as he concluded what was an impressive story of the Lord humbling him and bringing him back to the Cross, he said, 'However I cannot say that I am filled with the Spirit yet, but I am seeking'.

Afterwards I drew him aside and said, 'While I praise God for your testimony I was disappointed to hear you say that you are not yet filled with the Spirit.' As we talked further, he began to see that he did not need to go any further than the Cross to be filled with the Spirit. In that place of brokenness where the Blood was applied to his heart, Jesus was made to him all he needed. And inasmuch as he had come to the Cross, God did indeed fill him with the Spirit because of the Blood of Christ—if his faith would receive it. There he began to believe in the value of the

Blood of Jesus on his behalf. In those days he could be seen in quiet corners under the trees and elsewhere, bowed in wonder and worship, believing it all—cleansed in the Blood, therefore filled with the Spirit, and Jesus made to him all he needed, his righteousness with God and his holiness within. He returned to his station radiant, emancipated. As he humbly gave his testimony there, the Lord began to use his testimony to make others hungry. Christians began to repent and others began to seek Christ for the first time. He wrote back. 'It's rivers of living water again.'

How simple and how well within our reach is God's way of being filled with His Spirit.

CHAPTER SEVEN

BE FILLED AND BE FILLED NOW!

*'And be not drunk with wine, wherein is excess; but be filled
with the Spirit;*

*Speaking to yourselves in psalms and hymns and spiritual songs,
singing and making melody in your heart to the Lord;*

*Giving thanks always for all things unto God and the Father in
the name of our Lord Jesus Christ;*

Submitting yourselves one to another in the fear of God.'

Eph. 5. 18–21.

LET us look more closely at this great apostolic word, 'Be filled
with the Spirit' and let us note the grammar involved in that
word 'be filled', for it has helpful lessons to teach us. First it is in
the *imperative mood,* that is, it is a command. It is just as much a
command of God to be filled with the Spirit, as it is not to be
drunk with wine, which is the phrase that immediately precedes
it. If we are not cleansed by the Blood of Christ and filled with
God's Spirit, we are disobeying God. To be filled with the Spirit
is not optional, but obligatory on every Christian, whether a
housewife, a business man or a preacher. Indeed that fulness is
as much commanded at the sink as in the pulpit, and it is not
commanded for our compliance at some future date, but *now!*

Secondly, this verb 'be filled' is in the *passive voice.* It is not
fill yourself, but be filled. It is something that is done to us, not
something we can do ourselves. This implies that all we have to
offer is emptiness. If only we were more content to take that
position before God, we would be more often filled; instead of
which, we are all the time making attempts to come other than as
empty sinners and to meet our own needs, when we should be
letting Him do it. Being filled with the Spirit is not an attain-

ment, but an 'obtainment', obtained through simple faith by those who know and acknowledge their emptiness. They were saved by grace without works, and they expect to be filled on the same principle. Nowhere is the necessity for us to present only our emptiness better expressed than in Mary Shackleton's lovely hymn, two verses of which read:

> *But though I cannot sing, or tell, or know*
> *The fulness of Thy love, while here below,*
> *My empty vessel I may freely bring;*
> *Oh Thou, who art of love the living spring,*
> *My vessel fill.*

> *I am an empty vessel, not one thought*
> *Or look of love I ever to Thee brought,*
> *But I may come and come again to Thee*
> *With this the empty sinner's only plea,*
> *Thou lovest me.*

A word of testimony may help here. On one occasion there had been real defeat in my walk as a Christian and I was much oppressed with a sense of failure. I turned idly to a notebook of mine, and saw two words which I had scribbled there some time before, 'Be filled'. They seemed to come as a direct word from God to me.

'But Lord,' I said, 'I am such a failure.'

'I know,' He replied, 'but be filled.'

'But not so soon after defeat,' I said, 'I must surely improve first.'

'You need do nothing of the sort first,' He said, 'Be filled and be filled now.'

'But how can I when I feel so oppressed with my sin?'

'The Blood of Jesus cleanseth from all sin,' He replied patiently. 'Be filled and be filled now!'

Be filled, be filled, be filled was all that came back to me in reply to every doubtful thought. This was the last message I would have expected from God that day. To go from the lowest to the highest so immediately seemed impossible. But when I saw the power of the Blood of Jesus to cleanse completely, I could only bow my head and say 'Amen, Lord' to both His command and promise, and receive the cleansing and the filling. A day of rich blessing followed and others got something of the overflow.

The simple truth is that the fulness of the Holy Spirit is not merely for super-saints who by their consecration and devotedness may be deemed to have qualified, but sinners and failures who have learnt to repent and who see the perfect, present cleansing available to them in the Blood of Jesus. Thank God, whereas this word is in the imperative mood, it is in the passive voice. This simply means that 'it is of faith, that it might be by grace', and this in turn means that 'the promise might be sure to all the seed' (Rom. 4. 16), not only to saints of high attainments, but to feeble, failing people like some of us. Grace by its very nature makes the promise sure to failures who admit their failure, and they can do that *now*. Someone has said, 'The Spirit's fulness is not the reward of our faithfulness, but God's gift for our defeat'. He was not given to the disciples in Acts 28 as the culmination and reward of their wonderful service, but in Acts 2 when they had proved themselves cowards, meeting behind barred doors.

There is, therefore, no need to struggle for self-improvement first, for that is to seek the Holy Spirit 'not by faith, but, as it were by the works of the law' (Rom. 9. 32). Nor is there any need to wait for Him, as some have thought—no need to wait, that is to say, any longer than it takes us to be willing to call sin, sin and come to the Cross with it. The Holy Spirit has already been given. True, the disciples were of old told, 'Tarry ye in the city of Jerusalem, until ye be endued with power from on high' (Luke 24. 49) but that was because the historic moment of the giving of the Holy Spirit had not yet come. But now that He is given, all may be filled—and filled *now*.

The third thing to note about the word 'be filled' is that it is in the *present continuous tense*. This, of course, is not apparent in the English translation. Indeed in the English language we do not use the present continuous tense at all. In the Greek, however, this word here, 'be filled', is literally 'be being filled'. In other words, it is not a command that we be filled once-for-all or even occasionally, but that we be filled continually. It is not a static experience. The figure the Lord Jesus uses of the fulness of the Spirit in John 4 is of a spring of water leaping up in us. 'The water that I shall give him will become in him a spring of water welling up unto eternal life' (v. 14, R.S.V.). There is nothing very static about that!

The fact that we are to go on being filled with the Spirit is of tremendous importance, and I would beg the reader to give special attention to this point. Unless we go on being filled with the Spirit, the great initial experience by which we may have begun will become but a memory of the past, while in the present we are empty, defeated and dry. Indeed it is a sad and rather depressing thing to hear a man tell of a past filling, if he cannot tell you of a present one too. The fact of his silence about the present is often an indication that nothing is happening in the present. Indeed I had better be silent about my testimony of what happened further back in the past, if I have not a testimony of His fulness right now in the present.

The honest fact is that sometimes nothing is happening in the present with us, in spite of all our experience in the past. The blessing is ours today as we continue in His light today. But one refusal of the light, one refusal to accept conviction at any point, however small, will block the flow of the Spirit. But the command, 'be filled', that came to us yesterday comes to us again today in our present condition; and the Blood that cleansed us yesterday will cleanse us today, if we will repent today, and the Lord Jesus who filled our cups to overflowing yesterday will do the same today. Our need for a continuous filling with the Spirit is matched by the continuous cleansing from sin which the Blood of Christ imparts. Indeed 1 John 1. 7 has another of these hidden present continuous tenses. It should read, 'If we walk in the light, as he is in the light . . . the blood of Jesus Christ, His Son *goes on cleansing us* from all sin.' This continuous cleansing is, however, not automatic; it only goes on cleansing as we go on walking in the light, that is, go on saying 'yes' to what that light reveals, which in turn means go on repenting.

A lady missionary from East Africa told me how she was

greeted once by one of the African Christian leaders who asked her, 'Are you praising the Lord this morning, sister?'

'If you want to know the truth I'm not,' she replied, 'not this morning.'

'Why is that?' he asked.

After a moment's hesitation she replied softly, 'I lost my temper in my bungalow this morning.'

All he answered was, 'Has the Blood of Jesus lost its power?' and quietly passed on. That was just the message she needed. She saw it had indeed not lost its power and it was not long before she had come to the Lord in repentance and been cleansed and filled afresh, with a consequent new testimony of praise to Him.

Even the most outstanding initial experience of being filled with the Spirit can only be maintained by a constant readiness to be cleansed in the Blood of Christ from the smallest things as they come. Without such continuous cleansing and continuous fulness, the great initial experience will become little more than a sad memory, which only accuses us of our present emptiness and coldness. Indeed a conspicuous experience in the past has sometimes proved to be a life-long liability to a man, for he is always haunted by the memory of that experience which in spite of his struggles, he cannot regain. But if we are willing to 'walk in the light, as He is in the light', saying yes quickly to all that that light reveals as sin, the Blood of Jesus will keep on cleansing us from all sin, grace will restore what sin has taken away and our experience of the Spirit's fulness will be fresh and up-to-date.

All this has many important implications—one of them being in the matter of fellowship. The fact that some Christians have had an experience of the gifts of the Spirit (speaking in tongues, healing and the like) and some have not, has sometimes imposed a strain on their fellowship one with another. The fact that a man has had an experience of the gifts of the Spirit will not of itself prevent sin coming into his heart, and once it has come, no harking back to those past experiences or endeavouring to gain new ones will restore peace. For that he must come to the Cross of the Lord Jesus as a sinner, as empty as if he had never had any great experiences. Nothing but the Blood of Jesus can wash away his stain and make him whole again. There he will meet others who have likewise found the inability of their respective doctrinal backgrounds to help them in their time of need and who are repenting at the Cross. There is not a thing to choose between the whole lot of them! They are just a bunch of sinners, but sinners who are finding for that very reason the middle walls of partition between them broken down and themselves having fellowship with one another. If we were only willing to live more on the basis of a 'now' relationship with God, we would find the fancied ground of our superiority to one another crumbling beneath our feet. In the 'now' we would have to confess sometimes that things had gone wrong with us, and in the 'now' would have to find our way to the feet of Jesus for restoration. There we would find ourselves drawn in love to others who were being equally honest.

No harking back to past experiences, then, can take the place of this honest dealing with God in the present. But this dealing with God is not all repentance, it is faith too. And faith, as someone has said, is not asking for what we have not got, but making use of what God says we have. It is our response simply to God's Word. The Word comes to us and faith believes and says, 'Thank You, Lord'. But the Word has got to come to us, or else faith is merely an effort of our own. To illustrate I may quote my experience in writing this book. As I was at work on the earlier part my mind seemed dull and lifeless and my heart uninspired. I said to myself, 'If ever there was a time when I did not feel filled with the Spirit, it is now. And yet I am trying to write about it.' In that condition I was tempted to strive in prayer and ask God desperately for what I felt I did not have. But mercifully I just had not the strength to do any such agonising. Along that line I felt defeated before I began. I felt too that to go hunting round in my heart for something to repent of would also be mere self-effort. At an end of myself, I could only tell the Lord my condition. That morning in my reading, God's Word *came* to me; it was the first text in Daily Light for December 2nd. 'Ye have an unction from the Holy One, and ye know all things' (1 John 2. 20). God said I *had* it. As I turned to my Bible and read further, I saw that the passage referred to went on to say, 'And as for you, the anointing which ye received of him abideth in you' (v. 27, R.V.). I saw that He said that the anointing I had received of Him, abides, or to use another word, remains, and does not change. It was God who said I had this and it did not change. I did not have to think it up, it was God's given word to me in my needy condition. How safe, then, to turn from my feelings or lack of them, to receive the Word and say, 'Thank you, Lord!' And how quickly new life, enlargement of heart and help came to me from the Holy Spirit. I saw again the truth that faith is not asking for what we have not got but making use of what God says we have.

I give it as my experience that I have never come out of cold-ness and deadness except by faith. For even where repentance seems to be the dominant act, there yet has to be faith. Never has deliverance come by some longed-for climactic experience sud-denly hitting me. There has certainly been the longing for some such experience and the praying for it. But the feebleness of my desires and of my praying has made me despair and give up ere I had begun. Then came His word, declaring some blessed fact of grace, then faith believing it to be true, followed by God's per-formance of that which was declared and promised, so that one could say at the end, 'He hath both spoken unto me, and himself hath done it' (Isa. 38. 15). Experiences, there have been, plenty of them, but invariably following faith.

In the light of all these rich provisions of His grace, do we not hear Him say to us:

BE FILLED AND BE FILLED NOW!

CHAPTER EIGHT

THE CONSEQUENCES OF THE SPIRIT'S FULNESS

HAVING considered the Apostle's word, 'Be filled with the Spirit', we must now pass on to consider the rest of the passage, which goes on to describe the filling of the Spirit as to its consequences. The results are delineated in detail, but they are not the results sometimes associated in our minds with the fulness of the Holy Spirit. Nothing is said here of the Spirit making us wonderful preachers, or spectacular Christians in some special way. The results mentioned seem much more earth-bound than that; and it is well that it is so, for many of us may never be given by God outstanding spheres of service. His work is to make us *normal*, so that we walk with Him all our days in what seem to be the most ordinary paths.

The first result of being filled with the Spirit is a *song of praise to the Lord in the heart*. The words that immediately follow 'be filled with the Spirit', are 'speaking to yourselves in psalms and hymns and spiritual songs, singing and making melody in your heart to the Lord' (Eph. 5. 19). I think that means overflowing with praise and testimony to the Lord Jesus, for a newly filled person is full of Jesus! And such melody-making in the heart to the Lord can be just as real in the kitchen as in the minister's study! Indeed there is more victory in the kitchen, where a wife has learnt to walk with the Lord Jesus, than there is in the study, where a minister has not. This melody-making, however, is thoroughly rational; it is not merely the result of an emotional uplift. The fulness of the Spirit means nothing, if it does not mean the Spirit showing us continually Jesus in His various aspects, enough for all our needs; our vision is just full of Christ and of His grace, and we cannot help but sing. As Charles Wesley puts it:

My heart is full of Christ
 And longs its glorious Master to declare;
Of Him I make my loftier songs
 I cannot from His praise forbear.

This is precisely what followed as one of the first consequences of the coming of the Holy Spirit on the Day of Pentecost. 'We do hear them speak in our tongues the wonderful works of God' (Acts 2. 11), was what the hearers said that day. The fact that the disciples were speaking in other languages was quite incidental. The important thing was the subject of their speech, and that was 'the wonderful works of God'. Praise to God was what they were engaged in, and that because the Holy Spirit had shown them Jesus risen from the dead, standing at the right hand of God for them, ready to give repentance to Israel and remission of sins. It was the wonder of the grace of God in all this that evoked their praise to God that day. It was basically a simple fulfilment of the promise of the Lord, 'He shall glorify me: for he shall receive of mine, and shall shew it unto you.' Their praise, their joy, their boldness were all the consequence of what they were given to see by the Spirit. Their speaking in other tongues was also the result of what they saw. Their hearts were so full of the vision of Jesus that they went beyond the bounds of speech known to them in their praise to God, and it became a sign to all those gathered at Jerusalem. The miraculous speaking in other languages would have been utterly insignificant had they not been expressing what the Spirit was revealing to them of Jesus.

So often in our thinking we associate being filled with the Holy Spirit with inspiring sensations, ecstatic joy and the ability to praise God with a new boldness and freedom, and to do so, sometimes, in other tongues. We can come to regard these as the principal things to expect, and seek them accordingly. It cannot be too strongly emphasised that they are not the Spirit's principal gift to us. His principal gift to us is to take of the things of Christ and show them unto us. Joy and praise to God follow as a simple consequence, for it is infinitely good news for helpless people like ourselves that we see in Him. The resultant praise can be in either a known or an unknown tongue. Paul said he would infinitely prefer it to be in a known tongue so that others can join in and receive the benefit of it (see 1 Cor. 14. 19), and we imagine most people would agree with him. If we make the mistake of seeking these things as His principal gifts, we shall be disappointed if we do not receive them; or in danger of making too much of them if we do. But if we are expecting the Holy Spirit to give us a new revelation of Jesus, we shall soon be 'speaking to one another in psalms and hymns and spiritual songs, singing and making melody in our hearts to the Lord'. Our joy will have a rational foundation, and we shall be able so to speak to others of what we see that they will be able to see the same, and join us in our rejoicing.

The second result mentioned is *thanksgiving for all things*: 'giving thanks always for all things unto God and the Father in the name of our Lord Jesus Christ' (Eph. 5. 20). This means seeing God in everything, and knowing that all the things that come to us, no matter from what sources they begin, by the time they reach us, come to us as God's permissive will, who works all things together for good to them that love God. That being so, they must be something for which to thank God, whether we see how they can be for good or not. Such an attitude of thanksgiving is quite impossible if we are proud and unwilling to give up our rights and our self-centredness to God: self-pity and complaining can be the only result in that case. But this precious thankfulness is closely associated with being filled with the Spirit, for God can only fill valleys, not mountains. Whether such brokenness, as submits and rejoices in all that God allows, is the condition or consequence of the Spirit's fulness, it is difficult to say. Probably it is both. In this passage it is given as the result of the Spirit's fulness. On the other hand, the lack of this submissiveness produces sins of self-pity, murmuring and doubting, which make it impossible for us to be filled, and which must first be confessed and cleansed in the Blood of Christ. Quite obviously, our repentance and cleansing on this point alone will have to be often reiterated; for whoever went through any of the severe tests to which we are all at one time or another subjected, without, at least at first, reacting in a self-centred way? But how gracious God is to restore our attitude when we acknowledge our wrong.

The third result mentioned, and this is perhaps the most important, judging by the amount of space allotted to it in the passage, is *mutual submission:* 'submitting yourselves one to another in the fear of God' (Eph. 5. 21). Whenever God speaks of our relationships one with another, the word He gives us is always 'submit', 'be in subjection'. In this passage, each relationship of life has this light directed upon it. Wives are to submit themselves unto their own husbands, as unto the Lord (Eph. 5. 22). What a searching word this is today, when 'petticoat government' is not merely a playful phrase, but a real fact; when bossing and nagging are an accepted part in our homes. But believers must confess this, if they are to be filled with the Spirit. Then Paul passes on to husbands. They are not called to submit to their wives, it is true, for Paul is at pains in other places to emphasise the headship of the man. But the husband is required to do something even more humbling; he is to love his wife 'as Christ also loved the Church, and gave himself for it' (Eph. 5. 25). Christ's love for the Church was a self-giving love, and the melting thing about it is that it led the Senior to humble Himself to serve the junior. In the same self-giving way, husbands are to love their wives. Though in Scripture they are the acknowledged seniors, before the Cross they cannot stand on their rights; and though senior, they are to give themselves to serve the junior, the weaker vessel, and to make her great, even as Christ did for them. How this strikes at male selfishness and male pride, and how surely must the believer confess it, if it should be manifested!

The same pattern of submission on one side and a self-giving caring on the other is seen in what is said with regard to the other relationships mentioned in the passage. Children are to submit to and obey their parents in the Lord—and I am sure 'children' here covers teenagers! Parents, on the other hand, while bringing up their families with godly discipline, are to avoid needlessly provoking resentment in their young people by their lack of understanding or harshness. Employees are to submit to their employers, doing them service as if they were serving Christ Himself. The boss on the other hand is to have a concern for the welfare of his employees, not storming at them ('forbear threatening'), knowing that he himself has a boss in heaven, who may well want to 'have him on the mat' as to the way he is treating those he employs. Mutual submission and caring in all the relationships of life is one of the consequences of the Spirit's fulness. The bending of the stiffneck is ever God's way for us if we are to enjoy a Christ-filled heart.

Let us, however, never lose sight of the fact that the way to be filled is not by trying to be more submissive or caring, but rather by repenting that we have *not* submitted to this one and that, and confessing that we have *not* loved them as we should. God reckons the Blood of His Son covering what we thus confess, and the Spirit fills where the Blood has cleansed, producing in us a sweet willingness to submit and love others.

Let us set out in full, then, this blessed and challenging passage, which gives us the cause and consequence of the Spirit-filled life:

'Be not drunk with wine,
Wherein is excess;

but be filled with the Spirit;

Speaking to yourselves in psalms
and hymns and spiritual songs,
singing and making melody in your
hearts to the Lord;

Giving thanks always for all things
unto God and the Father in the name
of our Lord Jesus Christ;

Submitting yourselves one to another
in the fear of God.'

Eph. 5. 18–21.